Table Of Contents

About Amazon Prime

Members of Amazon Prime enjoy benefits such as free and fast shipping for purchases that are eligible, the ability to stream movies, TV shows and music, exclusive shopping deals and selection, unlimited reading, and much more.

Shipping benefits are as follows:

- Enjoy **Free Two-Day Shipping** on eligible items to addresses in the contiguous U.S. as well as other shipping benefits.
- Addresses in eligible zip codes are offered **Free Same-Day Delivery**.
- Enjoy 2-Hour Delivery on as many as thousands of items using **Prime Now**. Always check if your ZIP Code is available. Visit Prime Now for more information.
- Enjoy **Free Release-Date Delivery** on pre-order items that are eligible delivered to ZIP codes within the continental U.S on their release date.
- **Free No-Rush Shipping:** You have the option to select No-Rush Shipping if you don't need your Prime order right away. Selecting No-Rush Shipping also helps you earn rewards.

Streaming benefits are as follows:

- **Prime Video**: Paid or free trial members from the U.S. and Puerto Rico can enjoy unlimited streaming of movies and TV episodes.
- **Amazon Channels:** You can watch your favorite shows and movies from HBO, SHOWTIME and STARZ channels without requiring a cable or additional apps as well as having the option to cancel anytime.

- **Prime Music**: Members in the US and Puerto Rico enjoy unlimited, ad-free access to hundreds of Prime Playlists and more than a million songs.

- **Amazon Music Unlimited:** Enjoy discounts for Amazon Music Unlimited monthly plans. Prime members can also enjoy exclusive annual plans.

- **Twitch Prime:** Enjoy exclusive discounts on pre-orders and new releases of physical games. Ad-free viewing for Twitch.tv users who has linked their Amazon Prime accounts. Furthermore, enjoy a free Twitch channel subscription every month as well as exclusive access to free game content.

Shopping benefits are as follows:

- **Whole Foods Market:** Prime members enjoy exclusive savings such as 5% back for eligible Prime members with the Amazon Prime Rewards Visa Card as well as 2-hour Delivery via Prime Now in select cities (with more to come).

- **Amazon Prime Rewards Visa Signature Card:** Eligible Prime members can earn 5% back every day on all Amazon.com purchases as well as rewards everywhere else you shop.

- **Amazon Prime Store Card:** Eligible Prime members can earn 5% back every day on Amazon.com purchases as well as access to exclusive financing offers.

- **Amazon Dash for Prime**: Amazon Dash Button ensures that you never run out of your favorite products.

- **AmazonFresh:** Prime members in select regions can receive FREE shipping on all Amazon Fresh orders of $50 or more by paying an additional monthly membership fee. They also can opt to pay a flat delivery fee for each order they place under $50. Go to AmazonFresh for more information.

- **Prime Wardrobe**: Prime Wardrobe is a Prime-Exclusive program that allows you to try before you buy from eligible items across women's, men's, kids' and baby clothing, shoes and accessories. You are allowed seven days to try-on the items at home. You will only be charged for the items you decide to keep.

- **Prime Pantry**: Prime members in select regions can shop for groceries and household products in everyday sizes and pay an additional delivery fee. Prime Pantry does not ship to addresses in Alaska, Hawaii and Puerto Rico.

- **Deals and Discounts, Compliments of Amazon Family:** Enjoy up to 20% off diapers, baby food and more through Subscribe & Save. Get 15% off eligible products from your baby registry.

- **Prime Early Access**: Be ahead with 30-minute early access to Lightning Deals on Amazon.com.

- **Amazon Elements**: Enjoy access to Amazon Elements products which is Amazon's own line of everyday essentials.

Reading benefits are as follows:

- **Prime Reading:** Prime users have the ability to borrow books, magazines and more from the Prime Reading catalog. They are able to read the borrowed content on their Fire tablets, Kindle e-readers or the Kindle reading apps for iOS and Android.

- **Amazon First Reads**: Enjoy early access for members in the U.S. when it comes to downloading a new book for free every month from the Amazon First Reads picks. Also enjoy exclusive prices for hardcover title purchases.

- **Audible Channels for Prime:** Enjoy unlimited listening to original audio series and playlists that are handcrafted for every interest.

- **Washington Post Free Trial:** Prime members have unlimited access to The Washington Post with a six-month free trial.

Other benefits are as follows:

- **Membership Sharing**: An Amazon Household can be created for two adults living in the same household to share certain Amazon Prime benefits. You can share your shipping benefits with your Amazon Business user account if you have a paid Prime membership under your personal account.
- **Prime Photos**: Enjoy secure, unlimited photo storage and enhanced search and organization features in Amazon Drive for you as well as the members of your Family Vault. Go to

Prime supplemental memberships include the following:

- **Amazon Fresh:** Prime members in select regions have the option to pay an additional monthly membership fee to receive **FREE** shipping on all Amazon Fresh orders of $50 or more. They can also opt to pay a flat delivery fee for each order they place under $50.
- **Amazon Channels:** Prime members can watch their favorite shows and movies from HBO, SHOWTIME and STARZ channels without requiring a cable or an additional app with the option of cancelling anytime. It's only $4.99–$14.99 per month for Prime members.
- **Prime Pantry:** Prime members in select regions can enjoy **FREE** shipping on all Prime Pantry orders of $40 or more by paying an additional monthly membership fee. They can also opt to pay a flat shipping fee for each order they place under $40. Note that Prime Pantry orders cannot be shipped to addresses in Alaska, Hawaii and Puerto Rico.

Note:

- Amazon Prime isn't available for customers who want to purchase products for the purpose of resale or to use Amazon Prime to ship products to their existing or potential customers.
- As per Prime Terms & Conditions, Amazon may change these benefits occasionally.
- Due to special shipping characteristics, some items are not available for Two-Day Shipping and instead will receive free standard shipping. Free standard shipping delivers within 4-5 business days.
- Prime Memberships may be subjected to sales taxes in some states.
- Customers who are guests of another membership aren't eligible for the benefits mentioned below unless they are eligible through their Amazon Household: Membership sharing, Kindle Owners' Lending Library, Prime Video, Prime Music and shopping discounts provided by Amazon Family such as 20% off on diapers and 15% off on Baby Registry Completion discount. Such customers are also NOT eligible for Prime Photos.
- Prime members who have been granted certain discounted monthly Prime offers can't share their Prime benefits with others.
- A Kindle device must be associated with the Prime account that's eligible for a particular benefit in order to use Kindle Owners' Lending Library.

About Prime Day

What Is Prime Day?

There was only a few days of the year to catch great discounts for your favorite products. Black Friday arrived every November as well as the January sales. However, there was nothing much to satisfy your bargain-hunting hunger through the rest of the year. The last three years have seen another bargain-filled day helping people save on everything from technology to home entertainment. That day is Amazon Prime Day!

Amazon Prime Day is simply a one-day-only shopping event. Unlike Black Friday, it's exclusive to Amazon and is only available for those with an active Amazon Prime account. Amazon Prime Day is a great opportunity for saving money on a massive range of goods such as electronic items as you would expect from one of the largest retailers in the world.

When Is Amazon Prime Day 2019?

Prime Day will take place on Monday July 15th at 12AM PT/3AM ET and will run through 11:59PM PT/2:59 AM ET Tuesday, July 16th. The sale will last 48 hours this year.

The lead-up period for Prime Day 2019 depends on the category you are shopping in. You must start watching out for early Prime Day Deals since there are different start dates for different categories.

What Kinds Of Deals Can You Expect?

Tons of items go on sale during Prime Day! However, certain items are more likely to see discounts over others. The following are the categories and products to watch out for in 2019 according to Amazon.

- TVs: now selling Toshiba HD 43-Inch Fire TV Edition Smart TV for $179.99 (for a $120 saving).
- Amazon devices: Amazon Echo devices, Kindle Paperwhite, Kindle Oasis, Fire tablets, Fire TV Stick.
- Smart Home: A wide range of products under this category will be marked up to 40% off.
- Video Games: Amazon has hinted about deals from Xbox, Oculus and Nintendo. It's worth checking out the deals on Nintendo items since they tend to be especially rare.

Can You Shop On Prime Day If You Aren't A Prime Member?

Technically, no. However, there are ways around it. You're eligible for a 30-Day Free Trial (https://www.amazon.com/amazonprime) if you've never signed up for Amazon Prime before. The 30-day free trial comes with everything that you would expect from the subscription including the bulk of the site's streaming options and access to Prime Day deals! If you are still a student and meet the same criteria, it's possible to get a 6-Month Free Trial (https://www.amazon.com/b?ie=UTF8&node=13887280011). Just make sure that you start it sometime in late June to ensure that the trial doesn't expire before the big day if you are going to use the free-trial method.

It must also be noted that Amazon usually offers discounted Prime subscriptions as a lead-up to the Prime Day. Therefore if you have already used your free trial, you should be able to get access to Prime for a lot less by catching that discount.

Below I will tell you how not to charge, if you do not want it for some reasons.

How Do You Get Lightning Deals From Amazon?

Lightning Deals (https://www.amazon.com/gp/goldbox) are sales with special Prime Day pricing. They usually offer a heavier discount, but as the name suggests, the deals come and go in quick time. Usually there's a limited supply of these items and given the amount of traffic Amazon gets even on a relatively slow day, the best can sell out before you are even able to get the item in your cart. Users are required to complete their purchase within 15 minutes due to the fact that they are so popular! Failure to do so, will result in the item in question put back on the market. You can join a waiting list for a specific item to become available again if the entire available stock of an item is sitting in shoppers' carts. You will receive a notification if the item becomes available.

The smartest move would be to head over to to the Amazon Deals page on the day of the event and sort by "upcoming deals." This will help you get prepared for a deal before it goes live. Being proactive this way however, doesn't mean you will be lucky enough to nab all of the savings you wish. You will be competing with thousands of people for a limited quantity of popular items. Manage your expectations and don't feel too bad if you miss out on something you really wanted.

Watch a Lightning Deal

You have the ability to Watch a Lightning Deal and receive a notification on your mobile phone when the deal is about to begin.

Follow the steps below to Watch a Lightning Deal:

1. Click **Watch this Deal** on an upcoming Lightning Deal.
2. You will then see that deal in the Watched Deals section of the Today's Deals page.
3. Your phone will receive a notification when the deal is about to start provide that the latest Amazon App is downloaded and notifications are turned on.

Note: You will only receive a single consolidated notification for multiple deals starting at the same time.

Claim a Lightning Deal

Follow the steps below to claim a Lightning Deal:

1. Find a Lightning Deal by selecting **Today's Deals** page on Amazon.com.

2. Search or browse. Then select **Add to Cart** for the Lightning Deal you want to claim.

   Note: The Amazon account that you use to complete your order must be the same Amazon.com account you use when claiming the Lightning Deal.

3. A timer will appear next to the Lightning Deal. It will indicate how much time is remaining to make purchases.

4. Once you add the deal to your Cart a timer will appear next to the Lightning Deal. It indicates how much time you have remaining to complete your purchase and redeem the discount.

5. Select **Proceed to Checkout**. You can find the promotional discount in the **Lightning Deal** section of the Order Summary before you place your order.

Note:

- Lightning Deal promotional discounts can't be transferred to other Amazon.com accounts.

- You may see a "Checking deal status" message after you select "Add to Cart" for certain very popular Lightning Deals. Amazon will verify eligibility on a first-come first-served basis before applying the promotional discount to an account for all Lightning Deals. Avoid reloading or refreshing the page in your browser while this status appears.

- A Lightning Deal will be marked "All Discounts Claimed" or "Sold Out" after all the promotional discounts have been claimed. You will have the option to go to the item's product page and purchase it at the current Amazon.com price.

Remember that the purchase will no longer be eligible for the Lightning Deal promotional discount.

- You won't be able to place an order for that same Lightning Deal again if you cancel your order, even if that Lightning Deal is still running.

Join a Lightning Deal Waitlist

Join a waitlist and be notified when a Lightning Deal becomes available.

The deal will be made available to the next customer on the waitlist if purchases in customers' Carts are not completed within 15 minutes.

Follow the steps below to join a Lightning Deal Waitlist to receive an alert if the deal becomes available:

1. Place yourself on the waitlist by selecting **Join waitlist** on a Lightning Deal.
2. You will receive an alert in the upper right-hand corner of your Amazon.com page indicating that the deal is available when you're next on the waitlist. A notification will also be sent to your phone if the latest Amazon App is downloaded and notifications are turned on.
3. Make sure that you add the deal to your Cart within the time remaining.
4. Now you are ready to claim the Lightning Deal! You will be removed from the waitlist if you don't add the deal to your Cart within the time limit.
5. Quickly complete your purchase to redeem the discount.

A waitlist will automatically expire when the promotion expires. Every customer remaining on the waitlist will then lose their chance of claiming that Lightning Deal.

The Join Waitlist button will only be active when there are spots available on the waitlist. The button is re-activated whenever a new spot become available on the waitlist.

Note: Joining a waitlist does not guarantee that the deal will become available for purchasing.

How Do You Know If A Deal Is Actually A Good Deal?

It's very easy to get swept up in the fast-paced excitement of Prime Day! It's important to stop and ask yourself whether you're getting a good deal like with all online shopping. Online retailers often use discount products to insanely low prices to make you to pull the trigger. Remember that not all price cuts are as they seem. Just because it says on the website that an item is at its lowest price, that doesn't always is 100% accurate. If you see a coffee shop claiming to have the best coffee in the whole world, would you believe them or scoff at their baseless claims?

Lightning Deals happen very fast. With all the hype and excitement, checking the specifics of the product that you're buying can go by the wayside. Reading customer reviews and Expert Reviews will help you get an idea about not only how good the product is, but also how old it is. The older a product, less valuable it becomes. If a budget laptop was $200 in 2011 and it is $150 now, it's a good idea to go for a newer budget laptop as they don't age well.

No matter what you will be buying, it's a good idea to read a few reviews and make sure whether there are more up-to-date, cheaper alternatives out there before you snap up what you feel might be a great deal.

Manage Your Prime Membership

Amazon Prime Price

New members will be charged $119 per year for an annual Prime membership and $59 per year for an annual Prime Student membership starting from May 11, 2018.

Existing Prime members with an annual membership will be renewing their memberships at a rate of $119 per year and Prime Student members with an annual membership will be renewing their memberships at a rate of $59 per year starting from June 16, 2018.

Monthly Prime members will continue to pay $12.99 per month. Furthermore, Monthly Prime Student members will continue to pay $6.49 per month.

About the Amazon Prime Membership Fee

Your card will be charged automatically for the next membership period at the end of the Amazon Prime free trial or your chosen membership period.

Your membership charge will be $12.99 per month if you choose to be charged on a monthly basis. However, if you opt to be charged on an annual basis, you will be charged $119 per year. Prime Video membership is $8.99 per month.

You have the freedom to cancel your Amazon Prime membership through Manage Prime Membership page (https://www.amazon.com/gp/primecentral) if you don't wish to continue your membership from a free trial to a paid membership. Furthermore, you are eligible for a full refund of your current membership period if you haven't used your Prime benefits.

Note: If your Prime membership is associated with a service that you receive through another company (such as Sprint), please reach out to that specific company for details about your membership rate and to manage your membership.

End Your Amazon Prime Membership

Click the "End Membership" button on the page below https://www.amazon.com/gp/primecentral/editMembership in order to end your Prime membership.

You are eligible for a full refund for the current membership period if you have paid for a membership and haven't used any of your benefits. The refund amount that you are eligible to receive will be shown before you confirm cancellation of your membership. It takes 3-5 business days for refunds to be processed.

Sign Up for the Amazon Prime Free Trial

Amazon Prime Free Trial members have all the same benefits as paid members.

Your account must have a current, valid credit card in order to sign up for the Amazon Prime free trial. You cannot use payment options such as an Amazon.com Corporate Line of Credit, checking accounts, pre-paid credit cards or gift cards.

Follow the steps below to sign up for the Amazon Prime free trial:

1. Go to Amazon Prime Free Trial (https://www.amazon.com/gp/prime/pipeline/signup).
2. Then click Start your free trial.
3. Follow the on-screen instructions that are prompted.

Once you are enrolled in the free trial of Amazon Prime, you'll have access to FREE Two Day shipping, Prime Video, Prime Music as well as access to the Kindle Owners' Lending Library.

Note: You won't be charged for your free trial. However, you will be automatically upgraded to a paid membership plan at the end of the trial period.

About Prime Video

Prime members can watch thousands of popular movies and TV shows at no extra cost. Use your TV, computer, tablet or mobile device to watch. You have the option to stream online or download for offline watching.

Go to Watch Anywhere (https://www.amazon.com/watchnow) and select your device to get started on the Amazon website.

You will be prompted to "Sign In" or register to connect a device to your Amazon account the first time you open Prime Video on a device.

You can download the Prime Video app from **Google Play (https://play.google.com)** *or the Galaxy Apps store for android devices or* **Apple store** (https://www.apple.com/ios/app-store/) *for IOS. Search for Amazon Prime Video, open the app detail page, and then tap* **Install**.

Sign In

Tip: If you or someone in your household has an Amazon Prime membership you are able to use that account information when signing in which enables you to take full advantage of Prime Video.

You can only link your device to one Amazon account at a time. You can create an account at https://www.amazon.com/account if you don't already have one.

On some devices you will be prompted to use a registration code to connect Prime Video to your Amazon account instead of a sign in option. Follow the on-screen instructions for guidance.

Note: It's important to remember that the registration code provided for your device is not the same as your Prime Video PIN.

Sign Out

You must Sign Out to remove your device from your Amazon account or to connect to a different account.

Follow the steps below to sign out from the Prime Video website:

1. Go to your https://www.amazon.com/gp/video/settings/your-devices.
2. Then find your device under Your Devices.
3. Click the Deregister option next to it.

Note: Most devices have a sign out option directly within the Prime Video app.

From the Prime Video home screen, first select **Help** or **Settings**. Then find the **My Account** or **Unregister Your Device** option and follow the on-screen instructions.

Follow the steps below to sign out from the Prime Video app for iOS:

1. Go to Settings
2. Tap My Account
3. Tap Sign Out

Follow the steps below to sign out from the Prime Video app for Android:

1. Open the Menu
2. Tap Settings
3. Tap Signed in as "Account Name"
4. Tap Sign out

Follow the steps below If you're using the Amazon Underground app to access Prime Video on your Android phone:

1. Tap the Menu button
2. Tap Sign Out and then confirm

Your device is no longer linked to the Amazon account you used to sign in once you sign out from Prime Video. You will no longer have access to Your Video Library and won't be able to watch Prime Video titles on that device until you sign in again.

You will usually see a prompt to sign in again on-screen once you sign out. Enter the information of your preferred Amazon account to sign in.

All of the movies and TV shows that you purchase from Prime Video are stored in Your Video Library (https://www.amazon.com/yvl). You have the freedom to access them on any of your connected devices.

How to Rent or Buy Prime Video Titles

Prime Video uses 1-Click ordering for all purchases. The purchase price is automatically charged to the default 1-Click payment method on your Amazon account when you buy a movie or a TV show from Prime Video.

You have the ability to rent and buy Prime Video titles from the Amazon website or your connected device once you have set your 1-Click payment method.

Go to https://www.amazon.com/gp/video/settings/your-account using your web browser to view or change your 1-Click payment settings.

Note: Prime Video is only available to customers located in the United States and U.S. territories. You need an Amazon.com account with a billing address and 1-Click payment method from an eligible U.S. location in order to purchase Prime Video titles.

Follow the steps below to buy or rent a Prime Video title:

1. First open https://www.amazon.com/av from your web browser or launch the Prime Video app on your connected device.
2. Browse featured categories or use Search 🔍 to find a specific title.
3. Select a title to open its video details.
4. Select More Purchase Options (or Prefer to buy? If you are looking at a specific episode).
5. Select Buy or Rent and then confirm your purchase.
6. You must enter your PIN when prompted to complete Prime Video orders if you have PIN on Purchase turned on in your Prime Video Settings.
7. You will see an option to Watch Now to start playback once your order is complete.

When you select **Buy**, you will be purchasing a video to own. You have the freedom to watch it anytime from Your **Video Library** on any of your connected devices.

When you select **Rent**, you will have a defined rental period to watch the video on any of your connected devices. The video will be automatically removed from Your **Video Library** as soon as the rental period comes to an end.

Note: The Prime Video apps for iOS and Xbox do not support video purchasing at this time.

- You have the ability to purchase Prime Video titles from the Prime Video (https://www.amazon.com/av) website or another compatible device and then access them from your Video Library within the Prime Video app for Xbox.

How to Pre-order Prime Video Titles

Visit Prime Video website to pre-order selected movies and TV seasons prior to their official release dates.

On Prime Video website you can find titles available to pre-order. Look for the "Pre-order" category under **Rent** or **Buy** to browse the current selection of titles.

Note: Pre-order purchase options are only available on the Prime Video website, not the Prime Video app on compatible devices at this time.

Follow the steps below to pre-order titles from Prime Video:

1. Go to Prime Video (https://www.amazon.com/av) on your computer or mobile web browser.
2. Then open the video details for the title you wish to pre-order.
3. Select the **Pre-order** purchase option.

You can usually find the release date for the title above the **Pre-order** button. The title will be added to Your Video Library at midnight Eastern Time or 9:00 p.m. Pacific Time on that day. You will also receive status updates including release date changes for your pre-order by email.

Your 1-Click payment method is charged for the order once the title is released. Amazon Pre-order Price Guarantee makes sure that the price you pay is the lowest price offered during the pre-order period.

Note: Go to Your Digital Orders (https://www.amazon.com/digitalorders) and select **Cancel Items** next to the pre-order title(s) in order to cancel a pre-order.

What is Your Video Library?

Your Prime Video purchases and active rentals can be found in Your Video Library.

Your Video Library is linked to your Amazon account. You have the ability to access it from any of your registered devices.

How to Watch a Prime Video Title

Follow the steps below to access Your Video Library:

- From your computer - Go to Your Video Library (https://www.amazon.com/yvl).
- From your TV, Blu-ray player or streaming media device - Open the Prime Video app. Then select Your Videos or Your Video Library from the menu.
- From your Android device - Open the Prime Video app. Then tap Video Library from the menu ▤
- From your Fire tablet or Fire phone - Open the Video tab. Then select Library from the left menu.
- Find the title you wish to watch. Then open the video details to view available playback options.
- Start watching a video from the beginning by selecting Watch Now. You will see a Resume option for videos you've already started watching.

Watch Prime Titles

Eligible Prime members can look for the **Included with Prime** or **Prime** categories on the Prime Video home page to find movies and TV shows which can be watched at no additional cost.

Watch First Episodes of Selected TV Shows for Free

Note that First Episode Free titles will include advertising breaks before and during video playback.

Open Prime Video and look for the **First Episode Free** category under TV shows to find such titles.

You will also see "First Episode Free" or "Free with Ads" messaging in the video details for TV seasons if this option is available.

Start playback by selecting **Watch First Episode Free**.

Note: You must need to make sure you are signed in to your Amazon account if you're using your computer's web browser.

Many of the TV seasons that feature First Episode Free are also included with Prime. Existing Prime members will be able to watch these episodes without ads at no additional cost. However, you will see advertising breaks during playback for First Episode Free titles that are not available to stream as part of your Prime membership.

Finding Prime Titles

Use the Prime Video page (https://www.amazon.com/av) on the website to browse Prime movies and TV shows.

Tip: Go to Prime Video (https://www.amazon.com/av) in order to browse Prime titles from your computer or mobile web browser.

Prime titles also feature a **Prime** logo or a **Watch Now with Amazon Prime** option in the video details.

If you're using **Search** 🔍 to find a specific title, you can also use the **Refine** or **Ways to Watch** filters to only show available Prime titles on many devices.

Download Prime Video Titles

Compatible Devices:

- Fire Tablets (Except Kindle Fire 1st Generation)
- Fire Phone
- Android Phones and Tablets
- iOS Devices

Follow the steps below to download Prime Video titles if you are using a compatible device:

1. First make sure your device is connected to a Wi-Fi or wireless network.
2. Find the Prime title you wish to download. Then open the video details.
3. Tap Download.

Note: Select the episode you wish to download and then look for **Download** ("down arrow") icon when downloading TV shows.

Select the **Downloads** option in the Prime Video menu in order to find your completed video downloads.

Download Availability & Viewing Periods

Note that only selected Prime Video titles are available to be downloaded. The time period you have to view a downloaded title while your device is offline varies with each title.

When the viewing period for a title is almost over, a notification will usually be displayed on-screen.

On-screen notifications will also appear if you have downloaded the maximum amount of Prime titles (across all the devices on your account). In such a scenario you will need to delete one or more titles to proceed with the current download.

Subtitles

You can turn on subtitles (" **CC** ") during video playback to display the audio for movies and TV shows as text on-screen.

Follow the steps below to browse titles with subtitles from the full Prime Video website:

1. Open Prime Video (https://www.amazon.com/av).
2. Look for the Search box at the top of the page. Then click the Search 🔍 icon to switch to search results view.
3. Scroll down to find the Subtitles browse filter in the left panel. Then select a language.

The results on the page will then be filtered to only show videos with subtitles available.

Most videos that support subtitles include English text. However, other languages may also be available. The available languages can be viewed under **Subtitles**.

Turn Subtitles On or Off

Follow the steps below to turn subtitles on or off:

1. Start playback for a movie or TV show that have subtitles available.
2. Select the Subtitles or CC option in your playback controls.

Customize Text Display

Follow the steps below to customize the text displayed for subtitles:

1. Go to Prime Video Settings – Subtitles (https://www.amazon.com/gp/video/settings/subtitles).
2. Use the Edit button to configure your presets. You have the ability to change the text color, style, size and more.

Turn on Audio Descriptions

Audio Descriptions have the ability to narrate information about actions, characters, scene changes, on-screen text and other visual content.

Look for rows on the Home page named, "Movies with Audio Descriptions" or "TV with Audio Descriptions" in order to find titles that support Audio Descriptions from compatible devices.

Audio Descriptions for Prime Video are available on the following devices:

*   Mac / PC Computers (Website Streaming)
*   iOS and Android Mobile Deices
*   Fire Tablets (2nd Generation and Higher)
*   Fire TV Devices (Fire TV, Fire TV Stick and Fire TV Edition TV)
*   Echo Show

Follow the steps below to Turn Audio Descriptions On or Off:

1. Start playback of a movie or TV show with Audio Descriptions available.

2. Then select the Subtitles and Audio option in your playback controls.

3. Select the audio track with the [Audio Description] tag or the desired audio language without the tag.

Video Subscriptions

What are Prime Video Channel Subscriptions?

Amazon Prime and Prime Video members have the ability to purchase third-party channel subscriptions such as Showtime, Starz and other streaming entertainment channels directly through Prime Video.

All of the movies and TV programming included with the subscription can be watched on demand on Prime Video devices that are compatible.

Requirements

You need an eligible Prime membership in order to start Channel subscriptions through Prime Video. Any one of the following membership types are eligible:

- Amazon Prime Membership
- 30-Day Amazon Prime Free Trial
- Annual Prime Student Membership
- Prime Student Free Trial
- Amazon Prime Free Preview
- Amazon Prime Fresh
- 30-day Amazon Prime Fresh Free Trial
- Amazon Household Shared Prime Benefits

If you were previously invited to share shipping benefits with a Prime member, Access to Channel subscriptions is not included.

Note:

- You cannot share channel subscriptions across Amazon accounts or Amazon Household profiles.
- It's possible that channel subscriptions may be subject to sales tax in some states.
- Channel subscriptions don't have any setup or cancellation fees. They also don't have a minimum duration. You can start and cancel them at any time as long as you remain an eligible Prime member.
- Premium channel subscriptions you have with your cable or satellite provider and standalone subscriptions you have purchased directly from the subscription provider are separate services. They cannot be used with Prime Video.

Find Channels

Look for the **Channel** categories and filters when browsing Prime Video.

The video details also include available Channel offers alongside other purchase and viewing options when you select a specific movie or TV show.

Subscribe & Watch

Select the **Subscribe and Watch**, **Get Started** or **Start Free Trial** option when you've found a Channel you're interested in.

Most Channels start with a free trial while the regular subscription period begins automatically as soon as the trial period is over.

Confirm your subscription details and complete signup by following the on-screen instructions.

Note: Subscription sign up is not supported by some Prime Video devices. You will only be prompted to get started on the Amazon website instead. You will also be prompted to sign up on the website if you receive shared Prime benefits through an Amazon Household. Go to Amazon

Channels Subscriptions (https://www.amazon.com/channels) to find and start Channel subscriptions from the Amazon website.

You are able to watch the movies and TV programming included with a Channel subscription on all your compatible Prime Video devices after you have started it. Simply open Prime Video and look for **Your Subscriptions**.

Most third-party channels feature live streaming enabling you to watch programming on supported devices the same time as the TV broadcast.

By default, Channels subscriptions will be charged to your Prime membership payment method each month on the renewal date.

How to Manage Your Prime Video Channel Subscriptions

View and manage your active video subscriptions from the Manage Your Prime Video Channels page in Your Account.

Go to Manage Your Prime Video Channels (https://www.amazon.com/myac) in order to view and manage your video subscriptions.

Note: Your Video Subscriptions is also an option which is available in the "Your Account" menu on the Amazon website.

You can find a list of all your active subscriptions as well as the monthly subscription price and renewal date on the Manage Your Video Subscriptions page.

Change your subscription payment method using the **Subscription Payment Settings** section if needed. You can also cancel your subscriptions on this page.

Note: You can't share video subscriptions across Amazon accounts or Amazon Household profiles. Your Prime Video devices need to be connected to the same Amazon account you used to start the subscription in order to access movies and TV programming included with a subscription. You can find Information about your registered Prime Video devices in your Prime Video Settings - Your Account (https://www.amazon.com/gp/video/settings/your-account).

How to Cancel a Prime Video Channel Subscription

Use the Manage Your Prime Video Channels page in Your Account to cancel your Channel subscriptions.

Follow the steps below to cancel a Prime Video Channel subscription:

1. Go to Manage Your Prime Video Channels (https://www.amazon.com/myac).
2. Look under Prime Video Channels and find the subscription you would like to cancel.
3. Select the Prime Video Channels option and then confirm.

The renewal date in your Channel details becomes the end date when you cancel. You will no longer be charged for the Channel each month. However, it's possible to continue to access the Channel through Prime Video until the end date.

Note: Prime Video Channels are not returnable or refundable after purchase like other Prime Video content. Monthly subscription charge can be stopped by Canceling a Channel. However, it does not generate a refund for previous subscription charges.

It's possible to reverse your cancellation request before the end date if you later decide that you want to keep the Channel. Once the end date is passed, you will need to start a new Channel subscription.

Prime membership is not affected by canceling a subscription. You can continue to access and manage your Channels as long as you remain a Prime member.

Changes to Your Prime Membership

You must have a Prime membership to access Channels through Prime Video. Any Channels associated with your account are automatically canceled if you no longer have an active Prime membership.

The renewal date in your Channel details becomes the end date once cancelled. You can continue to watch movies and TV shows from your Channel subscription until you reach the end date even if the end date is after your Prime membership is over.

About Prime Music

Have ad-free access to curated Playlists and personalized Stations, more than a million songs and albums at no additional cost for eligible Prime members through Prime Music.

Playlists are handcrafted collections of songs from Amazon's Prime Music catalog. Personal playlists can also be created by mixing your music and Prime Music. Prime members can also enjoy uninterrupted music and unlimited skips with personalized Prime Stations.

Prime members can play Prime Music on the following compatible devices that support Amazon Music:

- Echo Devices
- Amazon Music for Web (https://music.amazon.com)
- PC & Mac Computers
- iOS Devices (with iOS 9.0 and above)
- Android Smartphones and Tablets (v.4.4 and above)

- Fire Phone
- Fire Tablets
- Amazon Fire TV
- Fire TV Stick
- Amazon Fire TV Stick Basic Edition
- Roku Devices
- Bose SoundTouch Systems
- HEOS Devices
- BlueSound Devices
- Play-Fi Devices
- Sonos Devices

Prime members have the ability to download Prime Music for offline playback on phones and tablets with the Amazon Music app installed. Downloaded Prime Music can only be accessed within the Amazon Music app and cannot be exported.

The Prime Music collection of songs and albums is always evolving. New titles are added and some are removed to the Prime Music catalog often.

Note: You must have an Amazon account, a Prime membership, a billing address and 1-Click payment method from a supported country in order to access Prime Music.

You can download the Prime Music app from **Google Play** *(https://play.google.com/store/apps/) or the Galaxy Apps store for android devices or* **Apple store** *(https://www.apple.com/ios/app-store/) for IOS. Search for Amazon Prime Music, open the app detail page, and then tap* **Install**.

Where's My Prime Music?

Why is my Prime Music greyed out?

The reason for a Prime Music title to be greyed out in My Music or not being able to access it might be one of the following:

1. The Prime Music collection of songs and albums is always evolving. New titles are added and some are removed to the Prime Music catalog often.

   Songs and albums that have been removed will still be displayed in My Music. However they will be greyed out and no longer be available for playback.

   You can purchase it to regain access or if available, accessed as part of an Amazon Music Unlimited subscription if the song or album is available from the Digital Music Store (https://www.amazon.com/mp3).

2. You'll lose access to the Prime Music titles you have added to My Music if your Amazon Prime membership expires. Prime titles will be still displayed in your library. However, they will be greyed out and no longer be available for playback.
   You have the option to regain access by re-activating your Amazon Prime membership if the song or album is still available in the Prime Music catalog.

3. Amazon Music app will no longer be available to playback offline any Prime Music you have downloaded to your mobile device if you haven't used the app while connected to a wireless network in the past 30 days. You will see these Prime titles in My Music, however they'll be greyed out.
   If the music is still part of the Prime Music catalog, you have the ability to regain access to it by using the Amazon Music app while

online. Note that it may take up to 10 minutes to regain access to downloaded music after reconnecting.

When you sign out of the Amazon Music app, Prime Music you have downloaded for offline playback is automatically deleted from your device.

Note: You can only add a maximum of 100,000 Prime Songs to your music library.

About Offline Recommendations

Offline Recommendations are a collection of personalized Playlists downloaded to your device. With Offline Recommendations you have the ability to listen to music when if a wireless connection is not available or when you don't want to use streaming data.

The Amazon Music app creates a collection of songs based on music you have purchased and listened to in the past when you turn on Offline Recommendations. You can play this collection of music without using streaming data as it's pre-downloaded to your device. Offline Recommendations are available on top of the music you have downloaded to your Offline Library for playback without a wireless connection.

Offline Recommendations require a Wi-Fi connection and sufficient space on your device to download. The Amazon Music app disables further automatic downloads of Offline Recommendations if your device is running low on space.

You can only view your Offline Recommendations while your device is in Offline Music Mode. Tap **Settings** then switch Offline Music Mode from **Off** to **On** to enable Offline Music Mode. You can then view downloaded Offline Recommendations music by tapping **Browse**. You can remove the collection from your device by tapping the 3 dots on any Offline Recommendations collection. This action sends Amazon feedback that is used to improve your personal recommendations in the future.

When you disable Offline Recommendations, any Offline Recommendations music already downloaded to your device will be removed.

Download Prime Music for Offline Playback

You have the ability to download Prime Music titles to be played back offline on compatible mobile devices.

Compatible Devices for Offline Playback

Prime Music titles can be played back offline on the following devices:

- Amazon Music for Android
- Amazon Music for iOS
- Fire tablets

Note: You cannot download Prime Music titles to computers (via Amazon Music for Web and the Amazon Music app for PC and Mac) or any other devices that support Prime Music.

How to Download

Follow the steps below to download Prime Music titles from the Amazon Music app for Android or iOS:

1. Select the music (song, album, playlist, etc.) that you want to download.
2. Then open the **More Options** menu ("three vertical dots" icon).
3. Tap the **Download** option.

You can also turn on **Offline Music Mode** under **Settings** to show just the music that was downloaded to your device and is available for offline playback if you are using Amazon Music for iOS. Go to **My Music** and select **Online Music** to toggle to **Offline Music** if you are using Amazon Music for Android.

Tip: You can select **Recents** from the Amazon Music menu and open your **Downloaded** list in order to access your recent downloads.

Follow the steps below to download Prime Music titles on your Fire tablet:

1. Press and hold the music (song, album, playlist, etc.) that you want to download.
2. Tap Download from the menu.

Offline Playback Availability

You can download as many songs as you wish to from Prime Music to any compatible mobile device registered to your Amazon account.

You are allowed up to four different devices authorized to use Amazon Music on your Amazon account.

Important: You can only access and play Prime Music titles within the Amazon Music app. They cannot be exported to be used on other apps and devices or copied onto CDs and other external storage methods.

About Streaming Prime Music on Multiple Devices

It's only possible to stream Prime Music on one of your devices at a time.

In the event of you already streaming Prime Music on one of your devices and then starting streaming Prime Music from another device at the same time, you will be displayed a notification asking whether you would like to continue streaming from the new device instead of the current one.

Select **Continue** to switch to the new device. Select **Cancel** to keep streaming from the first device.

Note: This only applies to streaming Prime Music. You can play downloaded music and stream Prime Music from another device at the same time if you have Prime Music downloaded to a mobile device.

You are allowed to download Prime Music up to a maximum of four authorized devices on your Amazon account. You will be prompted to deactivate the Prime Music downloads on one of your devices in order to proceed, if you try to download Prime Music to a fifth device.

About Audible Channels

Audible Channels come free with your Prime membership. Enjoy original audio series and playlists handcrafted to suit every interest. Start listening by downloading the Audible app.

Prime Stations are ad-free and personalized streaming music stations that you can use to discover songs from the Prime Music catalog. You are free to like, dislike and skip as many songs as you like.

Eligible Prime members can listen to Prime Stations as part of the Prime Music service. You can listen to Prime Stations using the devices below:

- Amazon Alexa Enabled (Echo) Devices
- Amazon Music for Web (https://music.amazon.com)
- Amazon Music for PC & Mac
- iOS Devices
- Android Smartphones and Tablets (v.4.0 and above)
- Amazon Fire TV Devices (Amazon Fire TV and Fire TV Stick)
- Fire Tablets (with Fire OS 4.0 and above)
- Fire Phone
- Bose SoundTouch Systems

- HEOS Devices
- Play-Fi Enabled Devices
- Sonos Devices

Note: Prime Stations are currently not available on Kindle Fire (1st Generation) and Kindle Fire (2nd Generation) devices.

Start listening by opening **Browse** from the Amazon Music menu and looking for the **Stations** category.

Start streaming Prime songs from a category by picking a genre, decade or artist and selecting. Genre and decade stations will play you a collection of songs from that specific category or era. Artist stations will play songs similar to the particular artist that you have chosen along with some of their best songs.

Add the currently playing song to My Music using the + option in the playback controls.

You can customize Stations playback by saving ratings for songs. Select the **Thumbs Up** icon in your playback controls if you the song that's being played and would like to listen to more music like it. Tap **Thumbs Down** to stop playing a song and remove it from the Station's song rotation. These preferences will be saved to your account and applied to all of your devices to enhance your experience.

My Soundtrack is a personalized station created based on what you are listening to and what songs you have rated with **Thumbs Up**. You can influence the music on your station by listening to songs that you like to be included and rating them **Thumbs Up**.

About Prime Rewards

When Eligible Prime members use the Amazon Prime Rewards Visa Card or the Amazon Prime Store card, they earn 5% back at Amazon.com. Furthermore, all Prime members earn 2% rewards with Amazon Prime Reload.

The Amazon Prime Rewards Visa Signature Card offers card members 5% back on purchases made at Amazon.com and Whole Foods Market exclusively for customers with an eligible Prime membership.

If you are already an Amazon Rewards Visa Signature Card member, you can check whether your card earns 5% back on purchases made at Amazon.com and Whole Foods Market, including Whole Foods Market 365 stores and www.wholefoodsmarket.com.

Go to Your Account (https://www.amazon.com/your-account) and then select **Payment Options**. To see how much you're earning on purchases made at Amazon.com and at Whole Foods Market, expand the details of your Amazon Rewards Visa Signature Card.

You still earn 3% back if you are an Amazon Rewards Visa Signature Card member and an invited guest who receives only shipping benefits from another Prime member. Join Prime or share benefits with an eligible Prime member via an Amazon Household to upgrade to 5%.

In follow instances, your Amazon Rewards Visa Signature Card account will go back to earning 3% back on purchases made at Amazon.com and Whole Foods Market, including Whole Foods Market 365 and www.wholefoodsmarket.com:

- Your Amazon.com account not having an eligible Prime membership anymore.

- You removing the Amazon Rewards Visa Signature Card from your Amazon.com account.
- You closing your Amazon.com account.
- You linking a different card account to your Prime membership.
- You using your Amazon.com account to apply for another Amazon Rewards Signature Card. Once you are approved for the new card account, it will earn 5% back at Amazon.com instead.
- You no longer being a member of an Amazon Household with an eligible Prime membership.

About Amazon Fresh

Amazon Fresh is a grocery delivery and pickup service available exclusively to Prime members in select cities. Prime members can get the benefits of Amazon Fresh for an additional monthly membership fee of $14.99.

How to sign up for the Fresh Add-on

You can check if delivery or pickup is available in your area by visiting Amazon.com/AmazonFresh.

1. Go to Sign-up for Amazon Fresh (https://www.amazon.com/afx/nc/primefreshbenefits/).
2. Select Start your 30-day free trial.
3. Follow the on-screen instructions that are prompted.

Prime membership requirements

Both free trial and paid members of Amazon Prime and Amazon Prime Student have the ability to sign up for the Fresh Add-on. It's not possible for the Members of the Prime Video monthly membership to sign up for the Fresh Add-on. Invited guests of other members as well as Prime household members are allowed to sign up for Fresh Add-on benefits provided that one of the primary owners has a Prime membership.

Signing up for the Fresh Add-on

Your monthly Prime membership and Fresh Add-on will be billed separately. Amazon Prime is billed at $12.99 per month and the Fresh Add-on is billed at $14.99 per month therefore a total of $27.98 per month. Annual Prime members will be billed $119 per year as well as an additional $14.99 per month for the Fresh Add-on.

You can switch to the monthly Fresh Add-on by visiting Manage Your Prime Membership (https://www.amazon.com/gp/primecentral) if you have subscribed to Amazon Fresh annually. By 2018, all annual Fresh members will be switched to monthly subscriptions.

Signing up for existing Prime members

You have the ability to sign up for a 30-day free trial of the Fresh Add-on as an existing eligible Amazon Prime member. You will be automatically upgraded to a paid monthly add-on at an additional cost of $14.99 per month at the end of your trial period although you won't be charged for the free trial. You are free to end your Fresh Add-on any time. You will not be charged if you end your membership during your free trial.

Paying for your Fresh Add-on

Your Fresh Add-on will be billed separately from your Prime membership. However, your preferred Prime payment method will be used to pay for both of them.

Note: Amazon Fresh does not deliver to dorms.

Note: All orders under $50 will incur a delivery free of $9.99.

About Prime Wardrobe

Prime Wardrobe is a Prime-exclusive program where you are allowed to try out eligible items suchas women's, men's, kids' and baby clothing, shoes and accessories before you buy them. You will be given seven days to try the items at home. You will only be charged for the items that you decide to keep.

1. Add Prime Wardrobe items to your Prime Wardrobe Cart. You must add at least three items with the Prime Wardrobe icon below: **prime wardrobe**

2. Place your Prime Wardrobe order. Although the process is similar, it's separate from the checkout for other items on Amazon.com.

3. Wait for your wardrobe. You will receive the items in 4-6 business days. The 7-day try-on period only begins once all the items in your order reaches you.

4. Try on your wardrobe. You are allowed a period of seven days to try on your Prime Wardrobe items at home.

5. Check out and inform Amazon what you're keeping. Mark what you are keeping and returning by accessing your order in Your Orders (https://www.amazon.com/your-orders) during the 7-day try-on period.

Note:

- You're only allowed to checkout once. If you change your mind:
- Marked keep on something you want to return: In the Online Return Center (https://www.amazon.com/returns), request return in for a purchased item.
- Marked return on something you want to keep: You can simply keep the item. Amazon will charge you when they do not receive it.

- You are charged for the full value of your order, if you haven't completed checkout by 11:59 p.m. Pacific Time at the end of your Prime Wardrobe try-on period.

1. Return what didn't work out. Use the enclosed, adhesive prepaid return label in your re-sealable Prime Wardrobe box or bag to return items you did not purchase. Prime members are allowed until the end of the try-on period to postmark returns at an UPS drop off location of your choice.

2. Wait for your return confirmation. You will be notified via email by Prime Wardrobe when all your return items have been received. Visit https://www.amazon.com/returns if you wish to track the process of your return package.

Note: Prime Wardrobe only accepts credit and debit cards that have expiration dates at least 90 days in to the future. Prime Wardrobe does not accept prepaid cards and gift cards.

About Prime Pantry

Prime members in select regions have the ability to shop for their groceries and household products in everyday sizes such as a single box of cereal using Prime Pantry. You can find low priced products and exclusive savings in the form of deals and coupons on Prime Pantry. You can choose between thousands of items available, including snacks, breakfast foods, beverages, beauty and personal care items and household products and save the trouble of visiting a store.

Prime Pantry customers are given access to an exclusive collection of thousands of low-priced items in everyday sizes. Customers can pay for shipping in two ways. Customers receive FREE shipping on all orders of $40 or more with a Prime Pantry membership. Save up to $58 per year in shipping fees if you order more than once a month. Prime Pantry customers can also pay a flat shipping fee of $7.99 for each order they place. Prime Pantry offers deals, exclusive coupons and special promotions as well.

Get Up To 20% off on Diapers, Baby Food and More

Prime members save up to 20% on subscriptions to diapers, baby food (excluding formula).

Follow the steps below to access the discount:

1. Join Prime by visiting www.amazon.com/family.
2. Then choose from diapers, baby food and more.
3. Click Subscribe Now on applicable items. You must have 5 subscriptions arriving on the same day to the same address in order to be eligible for the 20% discount.

Note:

- You will not be eligible for the additional 15% discount and other benefits provided by Amazon Family on diapers, baby food and more for customers with 5 subscriptions if your free trial is over and you have not joined Amazon Prime. You will continue to receive the current 5% Subscribe & Save base discount on existing subscriptions.
- Go to Your Subscribe & Save Items (https://www.amazon.com/gp/subscribe-and-save/manager/viewsubscriptions?) to change your delivery schedule or cancel.

- Creating an Amazon Household enables you to share certain Prime benefits such as 20% off diaper subscriptions with one other adult in your household.

About Prime Early Access

Prime Early Access is a feature that enables Prime members 30-minute early access to Lightning Deals on Amazon.com.

When advertised on pages other than the product detail page, Prime Early Access Lightning Deals will say "Prime Early Access". If a Lightning Deal (https://www.amazon.com/gp/goldbox) is a Prime Early Access deal, it will also be displayed in the "Add to Cart" box on the product details page.

Note that all deals are available while supplies last. Prime membership does not guarantee that you will be able to purchase a particular deal. There is a possibility that a deal could sell out before the end of the early access period.

About Prime Reading

As a Prime member you now have the ability to read as much as you like from over a thousand top Kindle books, magazines, short works, books with Audible narration, comics, children's books for absolutely free.

Borrow Titles from Amazon Prime Reading

Amazon Prime members have the ability to borrow books, magazines and more from the Prime Reading catalog and read them on supported devices.

Prime Reading allows Prime members to read from a huge collection of Kindle books, magazines, short works, books with audible narration, comics and much more for absolutely free. The available content changes frequently with titles being added and removed.

Note: Prime Reading on Amazon.com is currently available only for the U.S. customers.

A Fire or Kindle device is not required unlike Kindle Owners' Lending Library. Prime Reading titles can be read on any Kindle e-reader, Fire tablet or the Kindle reading apps for iOS and Android.

Use your Fire tablet, Kindle e-reader or the Kindle reading apps for iOS and Android to browse for most Prime Reading content in the Kindle Store. Please use your web browser to visit the Kindle Store and access the Prime Reading catalog if you are using any other device.

Note: It's not possible to read magazines from the Prime Reading catalog on Kindle Cloud Reader, Kindle for PC or Kindle for Mac.

Borrow a Title from Prime Reading

Follow the steps below to borrow a title using your Prime Reading benefits:

1. Go to the Prime Reading Catalog at https://www.amazon.com/primereading.
2. Locate a title that you'd like to borrow. Then view the product detail page for that title.
3. Select the option to borrow the title for free with Prime Reading. Then choose one of your supported devices.

Tip: It also possible to borrow the title directly from the Kindle Store using any Kindle e-reader, Fire tablet or the Kindle reading apps for iOS and Android.

You will lose access to your borrowed titles if your Amazon Prime membership expires or is canceled.

Return a Title Borrowed from Prime Reading

You can return titles from Prime Reading any time as they don't have due dates.

Follow the steps below to return a title that you have borrowed:

1. Go to Manage Your Content and Devices (https://www.amazon.com/mycd).
2. Locate the title you wish to return.
3. Click the Actions button next to the title. Then select Return this title.
4. Confirm by clicking Yes.

About First Read

The Amazon First Reads program allows Amazon First Reads members the opportunity to download a Kindle book from our editors' picks each month before the official publication date only for $1.99. Prime members will receive it for free! Customers are also allowed to shop editors' picks in hardcover at exclusive prices. New titles will be announced on the 1st day of each month.

If you have an Amazon Prime membership you are able to:

- Download the Amazon First Reads title for free. With Amazon Prime (including regular, discounted, free trial or invitee Amazon Prime memberships), you are automatically eligible for the Amazon

First Reads program. It enables you to download one title a month before its official release date for free every month.

- Shop for all six Amazon First Reads titles at exclusive prices in hardcover editions.

Locate Amazon First Reads on Your Device

- Fire tablets: Tap **Books,** tap **Store** and tap **More to Explore**. Then tap **Amazon First Reads**.
- Kindle e-readers: Select **Shop in Kindle Store**. Then select **Amazon First Reads**.

Subscribe to the Amazon First Reads Newsletter

Follow the steps below to subscribe to the monthly newsletter of Amazon First Reads:

1. Go to Amazon First Reads (https://www.amazon.com/firstreads).
2. Click Sign up for the monthly e-mail.

Unsubscribe from the Amazon First Reads Newsletter

Follow the steps below to unsubscribe from the monthly newsletter of Amazon First Reads:

1. Go to Your Account (https://www.amazon.com/your-account). Then click Email under the Email alerts, messages, and ads section.
2. Click Unsubscribe next to Amazon First Reads.

Note: Unsubscribing from the newsletter does not affect the eligibility to download one free book each month for Amazon Prime members.

About Prime Photos

What Is Prime Photos?

Prime Photos provide free online photo storage to Amazon Prime members. They are able to save and share unlimited photos on desktop, mobile and Fire devices.

Amazon Prime members get unlimited photo storage as well as 5GB of storage for videos, documents and other files for themselves. They also have the ability to invite up to five friends or family members to receive unlimited photo storage and collect photos together in the Family Vault.

Prime Photos can accessible using the following:

- Desktop Web Browser
- Windows or Mac Desktop
- Fire Devices
- iOS and Android Mobile Devices

Note: You are only allowed to use Prime Photos for your personal and noncommercial use only. Prime Photos cannot be used in connection with a professional photography business or any other commercial service.

The unlimited photo storage benefits associated with the membership will end if you cancel or do not renew your Amazon Prime membership. The size of all uploaded photos will count towards your Amazon Drive storage limit. You can review available storage plans by going to Manage Storage (https://www.amazon.com/clouddrive/manage) if the content you have stored exceeds your available storage limit.

What Is Amazon Drive?

Amazon Drive provides secure cloud storage for your photos, videos and other files while allowing access from your desktop, mobile and Fire devices.

All photos, videos and other files that you upload to Amazon Drive are securely and privately stored in your Files and your Prime Photos library.

Supported RAW File Types

The following RAW photo files from the camera models mentioned below are recognized by Amazon Drive and Prime Photos as a photo file. However, file preview is currently unavailable. Note that this is not a definitive list:

- **Nikon** (NEF files) - Nikon D1, Nikon D1X, Nikon D4, Nikon Coolpix A, Nikon E5700, Nikon AW1, Nikon D800, Nikon D50, Nikon D610
- **Canon** (CR2 Files**) - Canon 5D, Canon 1D, Canon 1D MarkIIN, Canon Rebel SL1, Canon 60D, Canon 5D MarkIII, Canon 1D MarkIV
- You are able to store the following photo format types with Amazon Drive and Prime Photos. However, Amazon does not currently support previews for ARW (Sony), CRW (Canon RAW CIFF image) or ORF (Olympus) files. Download it from your account and open it using the appropriate program in order to view this type of photo. **Tip: T**ry converting the file to a DNG (Adobe Digital Negative) if your RAW photo file isn't recognized as a photo.

Note: While Amazon Drive recognizes these files as photos, some of the information associated with the files such as the time and date the photo was taken may not be recognized.

Managing Files Using the Website

Upload or Search for a File or Folder Using the Amazon Drive Website

You are able to upload files and folders to Amazon Drive using a web browser on your computer, tablet or mobile device.

Follow the steps below to upload your files and folders:

1. Go to Amazon Drive (https://www.amazon.com/clouddrive).
2. Drag and drop files into the window or click Upload to browse your files.
3. Follow the on-screen instructions.

Note: The Amazon Drive web uploader requires HTML5, which is supported on Internet Explorer version 10 or greater, Firefox 4, Chrome, Safari (desktop) 6, Safari (mobile) 6.1, Opera (desktop) 12, Opera (mobile) 12 and Android 3. Take advantage of the full features of Amazon Drive by upgrading to the latest version of your favorite browser.

The option to upload entire folders is currently only available for Google Chrome (version 21 and above) and Microsoft Edge.

Follow the steps below to search for a file or folder:

1. Locate the Search box at the top of the page.
2. Type in file name, extension or folder name. Then press Enter on keyboard.

Note:

- The results will be based on folder and file names and include file extensions (i.e: .doc, .jpg, or .png).

- The search bar searches all the content in your drive. Not just the folder you are currently accessing.

Download Files from the Amazon Drive Website

You are able to download files and folders from your Amazon Drive to your computer.

Follow the steps below to download files directly from your Amazon Drive:

1. Go to Amazon Drive (https://www.amazon.com/clouddrive).
2. Select up to 1000 files or 5GB total worth of files or folders.

Note: The items are downloaded as a ZIP file when selecting multiple files or folders.

1. Click Download.
2. Follow the on-screen instructions.

Delete a File

Deleted files will be moved to your Trash folder list. They can be restored if required.

Follow the steps below to delete a file stored in Amazon Drive:

1. Go to Amazon Drive (https://www.amazon.com/clouddrive).
2. Select the file you want to delete.
3. Click Delete.

When you delete files from the Amazon Drive website, they will appear in your **Trash folder** list. You are able to **Restore** or **Permanently Delete** the files for a period of 30 days. All items will be permanently deleted 30 days after being added to the Trash folder.

Access Trash folder list by clicking the **Trash icon** 🗑 in the navigation bar on the left side of the Amazon Drive website.

Follow the steps below to permanently delete a file:

1. Go to Amazon Drive (https://www.amazon.com/clouddrive).
2. Click Trash in the navigation panel.
3. Select the files that you want to delete permanently.
4. Click Permanently Delete.

Recover a Deleted File

You are able to recover files from your Trash folder if they haven't been deleted permanently.

Deleted items will be added to your Trash folder. You are given 30 days to either **Restore** or **Permanently Delete** them. All items will be permanently deleted 30 days after being added to the Trash folder.

Follow the steps below to recover deleted files:

1. Go to Amazon Drive (https://www.amazon.com/clouddrive).
2. Go to the left navigation menu. Then click Trash.
3. Select any files or folders you want to recover.
4. Click Restore to restore the selected items to the same folders from which they were originally deleted from.

Share Your Files

You are able to share your files via email or by copying a URL directly from the Cloud Drive website.

Follow the steps below to share your files:

1. Go to Amazon Drive (https://www.amazon.com/clouddrive).
2. Select up to 25 files and/or folders.

3. Click Share.

4. Either share a link by clicking Get Shareable Link or Share by Email.

Note: When you share a folder you will be sharing all contents of that folder including any sub-folders it may contain.

When you share a Cloud Drive link with someone, that person can share that link with anyone else. Avoid sharing sensitive or private information.

Managing Files Using Desktop Applications

About Amazon Drive for Desktop

Amazon Drive for Desktop allows you to back up, upload, download and sync files on your computer without connecting to the Amazon Drive website.

The Amazon Drive for Desktop application is compatible with:

- Mac computers running Mac OS X 10.10 and higher
- Windows computers running Windows 7 and higher

Install Amazon Drive for Desktop

You can bulk upload files and folders to your Amazon drive account by installing Amazon Drive for Desktop. You can also use it to download files stored on Amazon Drive to your computer.

Amazon Drive for Desktop is compatible with computers running Windows 7 or newer and Mac OS X 10.10 or newer.

Follow the steps below to install Amazon Drive for Desktop:

1. Go to Amazon Drive (https://www.amazon.com/clouddrive).

2. Click Manage Storage.

3. Click Download your content with the Desktop App. Then select Get app.

4. Follow the on-screen instructions.

Note: You can find the Amazon Drive App for Desktop in your computer's taskbar (PC) or menu bar (Mac) as well as an Amazon Drive folder on your computer once it is installed.

Upload Files Using Amazon Drive for Desktop

Follow the steps below to upload files:

1. First select the files or folders from your computer that you want to upload.

2. Then move those files or folders into the **Amazon Drive** folder on your computer.

   Note: It is possible to upload individual files up to 48.82GB in size to Amazon Drive or Prime Photos. The maximum file upload size may be lower than 48.82GB due to limitations outside of Amazon's service in certain instances. This includes limitations with your web browser settings or specifications.

Tip: An upload can be paused by selecting **Pause**. Select **Resume** to continue uploading.

The newly uploaded files or folders will be automatically available on the Amazon Drive website. They are accessible from any connected Mac or PC computer.

Any changes made to these files or folders will be automatically reflected in your Amazon Drive (https://www.amazon.com/clouddrive). Changes made to these files or folders online will also be automatically reflected on your computer.

Download Files Using Amazon Drive Desktop

You are able to download files by using either the syncing feature or by selecting individual folders or files.

Follow the steps below to select individual files and folders to download without syncing:

1. Open Amazon Drive for Desktop in your computer's taskbar (PC) or menu bar (Mac) and click on .
2. Then click the Upload Icon .
3. Click the Downloads tab.
4. Click on Select folders button.
5. Select a destination folder.
6. Click New Folder and enter a name for the folder in order to make a new folder.
7. Click on Download to...

The files in your selected folder and any sub-folders will start downloading to the selected location.

Note: When downloading your files to the same location, Amazon Drive for Desktop will skip duplicate files found on the local disk. Amazon Drive for Desktop only downloads new files/folders that are already not located in the destination folder while downloading all content to the same location.

You may choose to delete the content from Amazon Drive once you download it to the desktop or external drive.

Follow the steps below to delete the content from Amazon Drive:

1. Start by clicking on the web icon ⊕ in the task bar menu of the Amazon Drive Desktop app.
2. Login to your Amazon Drive account.
3. Then delete files and folders that you no longer need to be stored on the Amazon Drive.

Sync Files Using Amazon Drive for Desktop

You can synchronize the Amazon Drive folder on your computer with the files in your Amazon Drive account online.

You can make changes to your files on Amazon Drive from the Amazon Drive folder on your computer with synchronization. This includes changes such as adding, moving, copying and deleting. The synchronization feature is set to On by default.

Follow the steps below to select or deselect folders to synchronize using the Amazon Drive Desktop application:

1. Start by opening Amazon Drive for Desktop in your computer's taskbar (PC) or menu bar (Mac).
2. Click the Settings icon. Then click Preferences.
3. Click Choose folders in the Sync tab.
4. Select the files or folders from your Amazon Drive that you wish to sync.
5. Click Sync.

Note: Amazon Drive for Desktop allows you to upload large files such as files larger than 2GB in size. It is possible to upload individual files up to 48.82GB in size to Amazon Drive or Prime Photos. The maximum file upload size may be lower than 48.82GB due to limitations outside of Amazon's service in certain instances. This includes limitations with your web browser settings or specifications.

Back up Files Using Amazon Drive Desktop

You select folders and set a schedule to automatically upload content to free up local disk space with Backup. You have the freedom to customize the frequency of the upload, the location and choose the files (photos, photos + videos or all files). Any changes made to the folder will be automatically updated in Amazon Drive at a schedule you choose once Backup is enabled.

Note: You will end up with two copies of the same file if it moves to a new folder after the backup is complete. The 1st file in the original folder and the 2nd one in the new destination folder on Amazon Drive.

Enable Backup

Follow the steps below to enable backup:

1. First open Amazon Drive for Desktop in your computer's taskbar (PC) or menu bar (Mac).
2. Then click the Menu icon (three dots) and select Backup.
3. Click Add folder.
4. Select the folder, frequency and the type of content you want to back up.

Pause Backup Schedule

Follow the steps below to pause schedule:

1. First open Amazon Drive for Desktop in your computer's taskbar (PC) or menu bar (Mac).
2. Then click the Menu icon (three dots) and select Backup.
3. Click the Menu icon (three dots) from an individual folder that is set for backup. Then click Pause.
4. Click Pause All to suspend all backups.

Delete Backup Schedule

Follow the steps below to delete a schedule:

1. First open the Amazon Drive desktop app in your computer's taskbar (PC) or menu bar (Mac).
2. Then click the Menu icon (three dots) and select Backup.
3. Click the Menu icon (three dots) from an individual folder that is set for backup. Then click Remove.

About Prime Photos Features

You can have up to five other family members and friends with Prime Photos.

Features such as Family Vault, enhanced search and filters and browse by People or Places are only available to eligible Amazon Prime members and users that have accepted an invitation to join a Family Vault. Prime Photos can be accessed through the website and through apps for Android and iOS.

Family Vault

The Family Vault is a digital photo archive that has been designed and built for family and friends. A Family Vault can consists of up to six members including the Prime account owner. The members of a Family Vault can collect photos and videos together. Each member of the Family Vault gets their own Prime Photos account. It includes unlimited photo storage and up to 5GB for videos and other files. The photos in your account remain private unless you add them to the Family Vault.

Note: It's only possible to be a member of one Family Vault at a time. It's also not possible to combine two separate Family Vaults.

Search and Filter Features

You can organize your photos based on the people that appear in them by using Prime Photos image recognition feature. It's also possible to label the people in your photos so that you can find photos containing particular people more conveniently.

Use search and filters to:

- Find faces and objects in your images and group similar faces or objects together (like dog or ball)
- Search for photos by the type of environment the photo was taken in (like beach or sunset).
- Find photos based on where they were taken such as a country, state or city level.

Note: The setting for "Location or Location Service" must be enabled on the device you are using at the time you take the photo for photos to appear in **Places**.

Your labels for people are private to your account. They are not visible to others, including the people in your Family Vault.

Note: Unless you are a resident of Illinois, Image recognition in Prime Photos is enabled by default. For residents of Illinois, image recognition is disabled by default. You have the ability to enable or disable image recognition from the Prime Photos website or mobile app under Settings.

Locate specific photos in your collection by searching for items pictured in them. Amazon's image recognition features allow you to:

- Search by people, events, locations or things.
- Refine your search by date.
- Organize photos into groups.

Note: The setting for "Location or Location Service" must be enabled on the device you are using at the time you take the photo for photos to appear in **Places**.

Unless you are a resident of Illinois, Image recognition in Prime Photos is enabled by default. For residents of Illinois, image recognition is disabled by default. You have the ability to enable or disable image recognition from the Prime Photos website or mobile app under Settings.

The owner of a Family Vault has the rights to manage the settings for image recognition of that Family Vault. Contact the owner of the Family Vault if you are a member of another person's Family Vault and want to change your image recognition settings.

If you disable image recognition:

- Unless you enable image recognition search, filter by People, Places and Things will not work.
- None of your photos will be deleted. However Amazon will delete the image recognition data from your photos.

If you re-enable image recognition:

- Prime Photos will re-run image recognition on your photos. The duration of the process will depend on the number of photos you have.
- Your photos and the image recognition data will still be available in your account if you delete the Prime Photos app.

Amazon does not share your photos or any of the data derived from the image recognition features. Labels and data are only used to help you organize and find photos in your collection easily.

Share Your Amazon Prime Benefits

Prime members are able to share certain benefits with the other adult in their Amazon Household. The benefits include FREE Prime Shipping, Prime Video, Photos Family Vault, Twitch Prime, other digital benefits and exclusive offers.

Both adults must link their accounts in an Amazon Household and agree to share payment methods in order to sharing benefits through Amazon Household. Each adult is able to keep his or her personal account while sharing those benefits at no additional cost. Go to the Amazon Household main page (https://www.amazon.com/myh/households) in order to set up an Amazon Household.

The following Prime benefits can be shared with the other adult in your Amazon Household:

Shipping Benefits

- Prime Shipping
- Prime Now
- Amazon Fresh (if the member is signed up for the Amazon Fresh add-on)

Digital Benefits

- Prime Video
- Prime Photos Family Vault
- Audible Channels
- Kindle Owners' Lending Library
- Amazon First Reads

Discounts and Exclusives

- Prime Early Access

- Prime-exclusive pricing on Amazon Music Unlimited and Kindle Free Time Unlimited subscriptions.
- Up to 20% off subscriptions for diapers, baby food and more, and 15% off on Baby Registry completion discount.
- 2% rewards every time you reload your Amazon.com Gift Card Balance with your checking account with a debit card that's linked.

The Prime Benefits below can be shared with any family member subject to age restrictions:

Prime Photos Family Vault: Prime members have the ability to share free photo storage with up to five people who are more than 13 years old. Each individual receives their own unlimited photo storage account. They are also able to view and collect photos together in a Family Vault. Photos remain private until you choose to add them to the Family Vault. Go to Prime Photos (https://www.amazon.com/photos/home?ref_=cd_auth_home) to send invitations to get started.

Twitch Prime: Twitch Prime is a collection of Amazon Prime benefits specially created for gamers. Prime and Prime Student members are able to share the on-Twitch benefits of Twitch Prime. Members have the ability to link up to four Twitch accounts to enjoy ad-free Twitch viewing and exclusive chat icons. Twitch Prime provides access to free games, in-game loot and a free channel subscription for the first user under the shared account who accesses each benefit. Visit Twitch Prime (https://twitch.amazon.com/prime) to link up to four Twitch accounts with your Amazon Prime or Prime Student account.

Note:

- Prime Music, Prime Reading, the exclusive discount on video games and purchased video subscriptions cannot be shared.

- Prime Student members and customers who receive shipping benefits from another member as well as members with certain discounted Prime offers are not allowed to share their Prime benefits.
- It's not possible to share Prime benefits with child profiles.